A

Puritan Catechism

With Proofs

Compiled by

C. H. Spurgeon

❦

Contents

I am persuaded that the use of a good Catechism in all our families will be a great safeguard against the increasing errors of the times, and therefore I have compiled this little manual from the Westminster Assembly's and Baptist Catechisms, for the use of my own church and congregation. Those who use it in their families or classes must labor to explain the sense; but the words should be carefully learned by heart, for they will be understood better as years pass.

May the Lord bless my dear friends and their families evermore, is the prayer of their loving Pastor.

C. H. Spurgeon

Part One

Questions

1 What is the chief end of man?

2 What rule has God given to direct us how we may glorify him?

3 What do the Scriptures principally teach?

4 What is God?

5 Are there more Gods than one?

6 How many persons are there in the Godhead?

7 What are the decrees of God?

8 How does God execute his decrees?

9 What is the work of creation?

10 How did God create man?

11 What are God's works of providence?

12 What special act of providence did God exercise toward man in the state wherein he was created?

13 Did our parents continue in the state wherein they were created?

14 What is sin?

15 Did all mankind fall in Adam's first transgression?

16 Into what estate did the fall bring mankind?

17 Wherein consists the sinfulness of that state whereinto man fell?

18 What is the misery of that state whereinto man fell?

19 Did God leave all mankind to perish in the state of sin and misery?

20 Who is the Redeemer of God's elect?

21 How did Christ, being the Son of God, become man?

22 What offices does Christ execute as our Redeemer?

23 How does Christ execute the office of a prophet?

24 How does Christ execute the office of a priest?

25 How does Christ execute the office of a king?

26 Wherein did Christ's humiliation consist?

27 Wherein consists Christ's exaltation?

28 How are we made partakers of the redemption purchased by Christ?

29 How does the Spirit apply to us the redemption purchased by Christ?

30 What is effectual calling?

31 What benefits do they who are effectually called, partake of in this life?

32 What is justification?

33 What is adoption?

34 What is sanctification?

35 What are the benefits which in this life do either accompany or flow from justification, adoption, and sanctification?

36 What benefits do believers receive from Christ at their death?

37 What benefits do believers receive from Christ at the resurrection?

38 What shall be done to the wicked at their death?

39 What shall be done to the wicked at the day of judgment?

40 What did God reveal to man for the rule of his obedience?

41 What is the sum of the ten commandments?

42 Which is the first commandment?

43 What is required in the first commandment?

44 Which is the second commandment?

45 What is required in the second commandment?

46 What is forbidden in the second commandment?

47 Which is the third commandment?

48 What is required in the third commandment?

49 Which is the fourth commandment?

50 What is required in the fourth commandment?

51 How is the Sabbath to be sanctified?

52 Which is the fifth commandment?

53 What is required in the fifth commandment?

54 What is the reason annexed to the fifth commandment?

55 Which is the sixth commandment?

56 What is forbidden in the sixth commandment?

57 Which is the seventh commandment?

58 What is forbidden in the seventh commandment?

59 Which is the eighth commandment?

60 What is forbidden in the eighth commandment?

61 Which is the ninth commandment?

62 What is required in the ninth commandment?

63 Which is the tenth commandment?

64 What is forbidden in the tenth commandment?

65 Is any man able perfectly to keep the commandments of God?

66 Are all transgressions of the law equally heinous?

67 What does every sin deserve?

68 How may we escape his wrath and curse due to us for sin?

69 What is faith in Jesus Christ?

70 What is repentance to life?

71 What are the outward means whereby the Holy Spirit communicates to us the benefits of redemption?

72 How is the Word made effectual to salvation?

73 How is the Word to be read and heard that it may become effectual to salvation?

74 How do Baptism and the Lord's Supper become spiritually helpful?

75 What is baptism?

76 To whom is Baptism to be administered?

77 Are the infants of such as are professing believers to be baptized?

78 How is baptism rightly administered?

79 What is the duty of such as are rightly baptized?

80 What is the Lord's Supper?

81 What is required to the worthy receiving of the Lord's Supper?

82 What is meant by the words, "until he come," which are used by the apostle Paul in reference to the Lord's Supper?

Notes

Notes

Part Two

Questions & Answers

1 Q. What is the chief end of man?

A. Man's chief end is to glorify God (*1 Cor. 10:31*), and to enjoy him forever (*Ps. 73:25-26*).

2 Q. What rule has God given to direct us how we may glorify him?

A. The Word of God which is contained in the Scriptures of the Old and New Testaments (*Eph. 2:20; 2 Tim. 3:16*) is the only rule to direct us how we may glorify God and enjoy him (*1 Jn. 1:3*).

3 Q. What do the Scriptures principally teach?

A. The Scriptures principally teach what man is to believe concerning God, and what duty God requires of man (*2 Tim. 1:13; Eccl. 12:13*).

4 Q. What is God?

A. God is Spirit (*Jn. 4:24*), infinite (*Job 11:7*), eternal (*Ps. 90:2; 1 Tim. 1:17*), and unchangeable (*Jas. 1:17*) in his being (Exod. 3:14), wisdom, power (*Ps. 147:5*), holiness (*Rev. 4:8*), justice, goodness and truth (*Exod. 34:6-7*).

5 Q. Are there more Gods than one?

A. There is but one only (*Deut. 6:4*), the living and true God (*Jer. 10:10*).

6 Q. How many persons are there in the Godhead?

A. There are three persons in the Godhead, the Father, the Son, and the Holy Spirit, and these three are one God, the same in essence, equal in power and glory (*1 Jn. 5:7; Matt. 28:19*).

7 Q. What are the decrees of God?

A. The decrees of God are his eternal purpose according to the counsel of his own will, whereby for his own glory he has foreordained whatever comes to pass (*Eph. 1:11-12*).

8 Q. How does God execute his decrees?

A. God executes his decrees in the works of creation (*Rev. 4:11*), and providence (*Dan. 4:35*).

9 Q. What is the work of creation?

A. The work of creation is God's making all things (*Gen. 1:1*) of nothing, by the Word of his power (*Heb. 11:3*), in six normal consecutive days (*Exod. 20:11*), and all very good (*Gen. 1:31*).

10 Q. How did God create man?

A. God created man, male and female, after his own image (*Gen. 1:27*), in knowledge, righteousness, and holiness (*Col 3:10; Eph. 4:24*) with dominion over the creatures (*Gen. 1:28*).

11 Q. What are God's works of providence?

A. God's works of providence are his most holy (*Ps. 145:17*), wise, (*Isa. 28:29*) and powerful (*Heb. 1:3*), preserving and governing all his creatures, and all their actions (*Ps. 103:19; Matt. 10:29*).

12 Q. What special act of providence did God exercise toward man in the state wherein he was created?

A. When God had created man, he entered into a covenant of life with him, upon condition of perfect obedience; (*Gal. 3:12*) forbidding him to eat of the tree of the knowledge of good and evil, upon pain of death. (*Gen. 2:17*)

13 Q. Did our first parents continue in the state wherein they were created?

A. Our first parents being left to the freedom of their own will, fell from the state wherein they were created, by sinning against God, (*Eccl. 7:29*) by eating the forbidden fruit (*Gen. 3:6-8*).

14 Q. What is sin?

A. Sin is any want of conformity to, or transgression of the law of God (*1 Jn. 3:4*).

15 Q. Did all mankind fall in Adam's first transgression?

A. The covenant being made with Adam, not only for himself but for his posterity, all mankind descending from him by ordinary generation, sinned in him, and fell with him in his first transgression (*1 Cor. 15:22; Rom. 5:12*).

16 Q. Into what estate did the fall bring mankind?

A. The fall brought mankind into a state of sin and misery (*Rom. 5:18*).

17 Q. Wherein consists the sinfulness of that state where into man fell?

A. The sinfulness of that state where into man fell, consists in the guilt of Adam's first sin (*Rom. 5:19*), the want of original righteousness, (*Rom. 3:10*) and the corruption of his whole nature, which is commonly called original sin (*Eph. 2:1; Ps. 51:5*), together with all actual transgressions which proceed from it (*Matt. 15:19*).

18 Q. What is the misery of that state where into man fell?

A. All mankind, by their fall, lost communion with God (*Gen. 3:8, 24*), are under his wrath and curse (*Eph. 2:3; Gal. 3:10*), and so made liable to all the miseries in this life, to death itself, and to the pains of hell for ever (*Rom. 6:23; Matt. 25:41*).

19 Q. Did God leave all mankind to perish in the state of sin and misery?

A. God having, out of his good pleasure from all eternity, elected some to everlasting life (*2 Thess. 2:13*), did enter into a covenant of grace to deliver them out of the state of sin and misery, and to bring them into a state of salvation by a Redeemer (*Rom. 5:21*).

20 Q. Who is the Redeemer of God's elect?

A. The only Redeemer of God's elect is the Lord Jesus Christ (*1 Tim. 2:5*), who being the eternal Son of God, became man (*Jn. 1:14*), and so was and continues to be God and man, in two distinct natures and one person for ever (*1 Tim. 3:16; Col. 2:9*).

21 Q. How did Christ, being the Son of God, become man?

A. Christ, the son of God, became man by taking to himself a true body (*Heb. 2:14*), and a reasonable soul (*Matt. 26:38; Heb. 4:15*), being conceived by the power of the Holy Spirit in the Virgin Mary, and born of her (*Lk. 1:31, 35*), yet without sin (*Heb. 7:26*).

22 Q. What offices does Christ execute as our Redeemer?

A. Christ as our Redeemer executes the offices of a prophet (*Acts 3:22*), of a priest (*Heb. 5:6*), and of a king (*Ps. 2:6*), both in his state of humiliation and exaltation.

23 Q. How does Christ execute the office of a prophet?

A. Christ executes the office of a prophet, in revealing to us (*Jn. 1:18*), by his Word (*Jn. 20:31*), and Spirit (*Jn. 14:26*), the will of God for our salvation.

24 Q. How does Christ execute the office of a priest?

A. Christ executes the office of a priest, in his once offering up himself a sacrifice to satisfy divine justice (*Heb. 9:28*), and to reconcile us to God (*Heb. 2:17*), and in making continual intercession for us (*Heb. 7:25*).

25 Q. How does Christ execute the office of a king?

A. Christ executes the office of a king in subduing us to himself, (*Ps. 110:3*) in ruling and defending us (*Matt. 2:6; 1 Cor. 15:25*), and in restraining and conquering all his and our enemies.

26 Q. Wherein did Christ's humiliation consist?

A. Christ's humiliation consisted in his being born, and that in a low condition (*Lk. 2:7*), made under the law (*Gal. 4:4*), undergoing the miseries of this life (*Isa. 53:3*), the wrath of God (*Matt. 27:46*), and the cursed death of the cross; (*Phil. 2:8*) in being buried, and continuing under the power of death for a time (*Matt. 12:40*).

27 Q. Wherein consists Christ's exaltation?

A. Christ's exaltation consists in his rising again from the dead on the third day (*1 Cor. 15:4*), in ascending up into heaven, and sitting at the right hand of God the Father (*Mk. 16:19*), and in coming to judge the world at the last day (*Acts 17:31*).

28 Q. How are we made partakers of the redemption purchased by Christ?

A. We are made partakers of the redemption purchased by Christ, by the effectual application of it to us (*Jn. 1:12*) by his Holy Spirit. (*Tit. 3:5-6*)

29 Q. How does the Spirit apply to us the redemption purchased by Christ?

A. The Spirit applies to us the redemption purchased by Christ, by working faith in us (*Eph. 2:8*), and by it uniting us to Christ in our effectual calling (*Eph. 3:17*).

30 Q. What is effectual calling?

A. Effectual calling is the work of God's Spirit (*2 Tim. 1:9*) whereby, convincing us of our sin and misery (*Acts 2:37*), enlightening our minds in the knowledge of Christ (*Acts 26:18*), and renewing our wills (*Ezek. 36:26*), he does persuade and enable us to embrace Jesus Christ freely offered to us in the gospel (*Jn. 6:44-45*).

31 Q. What benefits do they who are effectually called, partake of in this life?

A. They who are effectually called, do in this life partake of justification (*Rom. 8:30*), adoption (*Eph. 1:5*), sanctification, and the various benefits which in this life do either accompany, or flow from them (*1 Cor. 1:30*).

32 Q. What is justification?

A. Justification is an act of God's free grace, wherein he pardons all our sins (*Rom. 3:24; Eph. 1:7*) and accepts us as righteous in his sight (2 Cor. 5:21) only for the righteousness of Christ imputed to us (*Rom. 5:19*) and received by faith alone (*Gal. 2:16; Phil. 3:9*).

33 Q. What is adoption?

A. Adoption is an act of God's free grace (*1 Jn. 3:1*), whereby we are received into the number, and have a right to all the privileges of the sons of God (*Jn. 1:12; Rom. 8:17*).

34 Q. What is sanctification?

A. Sanctification is the work of God's Spirit (*2 Thess. 2:13*), whereby we are renewed in the whole man after the image of God (*Eph. 4:24*), and are enabled more and more to die to sin, and live to righteousness (*Rom. 6:11*).

35 Q. What are the benefits which in this life do either accompany or flow from justification, adoption, and sanctification?

A. The benefits which in this life do accompany or flow from justification (*Rom. 5:1-2, 5*), are assurance of God's love, peace of conscience, joy in the Holy Spirit (*Rom. 14:17*), increase of grace, perseverance in it to the end (*Prov. 4:18; 1 Jn. 5:13; 1 Pet. 1:5*).

36 Q. What benefits do believers receive from Christ at their death?

A. The souls of believers are at their death made perfect in holiness (*Heb. 12:23*) and do immediately pass into glory, (*Phil. 1:23; 2 Cor. 5:8; Lk. 23:43*), and their bodies, being still united to Christ (*1 Thess. 4:14*), do rest in their graves (*Isa. 57:2*) till the resurrection (*Job 19:26*).

37 Q. What benefits do believers receive from Christ at the resurrection?

A. At the resurrection, believers being raised up in glory (*1 Cor. 15:43*), shall be openly acknowledged and acquitted in the day of judgment (*Matt. 10:32*), and made perfectly blessed both in soul and body in the full enjoying of God (*1 Jn. 3:2*) to all eternity (*1 Thess. 4:17*).

38 Q. What shall be done to the wicked at their death?

A. The souls of the wicked shall at their death be cast into the torments of hell (*Lk. 16:22-24*), and their bodies lie in their graves till the resurrection, and judgement of the great day (*Ps. 49:14*).

39 Q. What shall be done to the wicked at the day of judgment?

A. At the day of judgment the bodies of the wicked being raised out of their graves, shall be sentenced, together with their souls, to unspeakable torments with the devil and his angels forever (*Dan. 12:2; Jn. 5:28-29; 2 Thess. 1:9; Matt. 25:41*).

40 Q. What did God reveal to man for the rule of his obedience?

A. The rule which God first revealed to man for his obedience, is the moral law (*Deut. 10:4; Matt. 19:17*), which is summarized in the ten commandments.

41 Q. What is the sum of the ten commandments?

A. The sum of the ten commandments is to love the Lord our God with all our heart, with all our soul, with all our strength, and with all our mind; and our neighbor as ourselves (*Matt. 22:37-40*).

42 Q. Which is the first commandment?

A. The first commandment is, "Thou shalt have no other gods before me."

43 Q. What is required in the first commandment?

A. The first commandment requires us to know (*1 Chron. 28:9*) and acknowledge God to be the only true God, and our God (*Deut. 26:17*), and to worship and glorify him accordingly (*Matt. 4:10*).

44 Q. Which is the second commandment?

A. The second commandment is, "Thou shalt not make unto thee any graven image, or any likeness of anything that is in heaven above, or that is in the earth beneath, or that is in the water under the earth: Thou shalt not bow down thyself to them, nor serve them: for I the Lord thy God am a jealous God, visiting the iniquity of the fathers upon the children unto the third and fourth generation of them that hate me; and shewing mercy unto thousands of them that love me, and keep my commandments."

45 Q. What is required in the second commandment?

A. The second commandment requires the receiving, observing (*Deut. 32:46; Matt. 28:20*), and keeping pure and entire all such religious worship and ordinances as God has appointed in his Word (*Deut. 12:32*).

46 Q. What is forbidden in the second commandment?

A. The second commandment forbids the worshipping of God by images, (*Deut. 4:15-16*) or any other way not appointed in his Word (*Col. 2:18*).

47 Q. Which is the third commandment?

A. The third commandment is, "Thou shalt not take the name of the Lord thy God in vain; for the Lord will not hold him guiltless that takes his name in vain."

48 Q. What is required in the third commandment?

A. The third commandment requires the holy and reverent use of God's names (*Ps. 29:2*), titles, attributes (*Rev. 15:3-4*), ordinances (*Eccl. 5:1*), Word (*Ps. 138:2*), and works (*Job 36:24; Deut. 28:58-59*).

49 Q. Which is the fourth commandment?

A. The fourth commandment is, "Remember the Sabbath day, to keep it holy. Six days shalt thou labor and do all thy work: but the seventh day is the Sabbath of the Lord thy God: in it thou shalt not do any work, thou, nor thy son, nor thy daughter, thy manservant, nor thy maidservant, nor they cattle, nor thy stranger that is within thy gates. For in six days the Lord made heaven and earth, the sea, and all that in them is, and rested the seventh day: wherefore the Lord blessed the Sabbath day and hallowed it."

50 Q. What is required in the fourth commandment?

A. The fourth commandment requires the keeping holy to God such set times as he has appointed in his Word, expressly one whole day in seven, to be a holy Sabbath to himself (*Lev. 19:30; Deut. 5:12*).

51 Q. How is the Sabbath to be sanctified?

A. The Sabbath is to be sanctified by a holy resting all that day, even from such worldly employments and recreations as are lawful on other days (*Lev. 23:3*), and spending the whole time in the public and private exercises of God's worship (*Ps. 92:1-2; Isa. 58:13-14*), except so much as is taken up in the works of necessity and mercy (*Matt. 12:11-12*).

52 Q. Which is the fifth commandment?

A. The fifth commandment is, "Honor thy father and thy mother: that thy days may be long upon the land which the Lord thy God giveth thee."

53 Q. What is required in the fifth commandment?

A. The fifth commandment requires the preserving the honor, and performing the duties belonging to everyone in their various positions and relationships as superiors (*Eph. 5:21-22; Eph. 6:1, 5; Rom. 13:1*), inferiors (*Eph. 6:9*), or equals (*Rom. 12:10*).

54 Q. What is the reason annexed to the fifth commandment?

A. The reason annexed to the fifth commandment is, a promise of long life and prosperity – as far as it shall serve for God's glory, and their own good – to all such as keep this commandment (*Eph. 6:2-3*).

55 Q. Which is the sixth commandment?

A. The sixth commandment is, "Thou shalt not kill."

56 Q. What is forbidden in the sixth commandment?

A. The sixth commandment forbids the taking away of our own life (*Acts 16:28*), or the life of our neighbor unjustly (*Gen. 9:6*), or whatever tends to it (*Prov. 24:11-12*).

57 Q. Which is the seventh commandment?

A. The seventh commandment is, "Thou shalt not commit adultery."

58 Q. What is forbidden in the seventh commandment?

A. The seventh commandment forbids all unchaste thoughts (*Matt. 5:28; Col. 4:6*), words (*Eph. 5:4; 2 Tim. 2:22*), and actions (*Eph. 5:3*).

59 Q. Which is the eighth commandment?

A. The eighth commandment is, "Thou shalt not steal."

60 Q. What is forbidden in the eighth commandment?

A. The eighth commandment forbids whatever does or may unjustly hinder our own (*1 Tim. 5:8; Prov. 28:19; Prov. 21:6*), or our neighbor's wealth, or outward estate (*Eph. 4:28*).

61 Q. Which is the ninth commandment?

A. The ninth commandment is, "Thou shalt not bear false witness against thy neighbor."

62 Q. What is required in the ninth commandment?

A. The ninth commandment requires the maintaining and promoting of truth between man and man (*Zech. 8:16*), and of our own (*1 Pet. 3:16; Acts 25:10*), and our neighbor's good name (*3 Jn. 1:12*), especially in witness-bearing (*Prov. 14:5, 25*).

63 Q. What is the tenth commandment?

A. The tenth commandment is, "Thou shalt not covet thy neighbor's house; thou shalt not covet thy neighbor's wife, nor his manservant, or his maidservant, nor his ox, nor his ass, nor anything that is thy neighbor's."

64 Q. What is forbidden in the tenth commandment?

A. The tenth commandment forbids all discontentment with our own estate (*1 Cor. 10:10*), envying or grieving at the good of our neighbor, (*Gal. 5:26*) and all inordinate emotions and affections to anything that is his (*Col. 3:5*).

65 Q. Is any man able perfectly to keep the commandments of God?

A. No mere man, since the fall, is able in his life perfectly to keep the commandments of God (*Eccl. 7:20*), but does daily break them in thought, (*Gen. 8:21*) word (*Jas. 3:8*), and deed (*Jas. 3:2*).

66 Q. Are all transgressions of the law equally heinous?

A. Some sins in themselves, and by reason of various aggravations, are more heinous in the sight of God than others (*Jn. 19:11; 1 Jn. 5:15*).

67 Q. What does every sin deserve?

A. Every sin deserves God's wrath and curse, both in this life and that which is to come (*Eph. 5:6; Ps. 11:6*).

68 Q. How may we escape his wrath and curse due to us for sin?

A. To escape the wrath and curse of God due to us for sin, we must believe in the Lord Jesus Christ (*Jn. 3:16*), trusting alone to his blood and righteousness. This faith is attended by repentance for the past (*Acts 20:21*) and leads to holiness in the future.

69 Q. What is faith in Jesus Christ?

A. Faith in Jesus Christ is a saving grace (*Heb. 10:39*), whereby we receive (*Jn. 1:12*), and rest upon him alone for salvation (*Phil. 3:9*), as he is set forth in the gospel (*Isa. 33:22*).

70 Q. What is repentance to life?

A. Repentance to life is a saving grace (*Acts 11:18*), whereby a sinner, out of a true sense of his sins (*Acts 2:37*), and apprehension of the mercy of God in Christ (*Joel 2:13*), does with grief and hatred of his sin turn from it to God (*Jer. 31:18-19*), with full purpose to strive after new obedience (*Ps. 119:59*).

71 Q. What are the outward means whereby the Holy Spirit communicates to us the benefits of redemption?

A. The outward and ordinary means whereby the Holy Spirit communicates to us the benefits of Christ's redemption, are the Word, by which souls are begotten to spiritual life; Baptism, the

Lord's Supper, Prayer, and Meditation, by all which believers are further edified in their most holy faith (*Acts 2:41-42; Jas. 1:18*).

72 Q. How is the Word made effectual to salvation?

A. The Spirit of God makes the reading, but especially the preaching of the Word, an effectual means of convicting and converting sinners, (Ps. 19:7) and of building them up in holiness and comfort (*1 Thess. 1:6*), through faith to salvation (*Rom. 1:16*).

73 Q. How is the Word to be read and heard that it may become effectual to salvation?

A. That the Word may become effectual to salvation, we must attend to it with diligence (*Prov. 8:34*), preparation (*1 Pet. 2:1-2*), and prayer (*Ps 119:18*), receive it with faith (*Heb. 4:2*), and love (*2 Thess. 2:10*), lay it up into our hearts (*Ps. 119:11*), and practice it in our lives (*Jas. 1:25*).

74 Q. How do Baptism and the Lord's Supper become spiritually helpful?

A. Baptism and the Lord's Supper become spiritually helpful, not from any virtue in them, or in him who does administer them (*1 Cor. 3:7; 1 Pet. 3:21*), but only by the blessing of Christ (*1 Cor. 3:6*), and the working of the Spirit in those who by faith receive them (*1 Cor. 12:13*).

75 Q. What is Baptism?

A. Baptism is an ordinance of the New Testament, instituted by Jesus Christ (*Matt. 28:19*), to be to the person baptized a sign of his fellowship with him, in his death, and burial, and resurrection (*Rom. 6:3; Col. 2:12*), of his being ingrafted into him (*Gal. 3:27*), of remission of sins (*Mk. 1:4; Acts 22:16*), and of his giving up himself to God through Jesus Christ, to live and walk in newness of life (*Rom. 6:4-5*).

76 Q. To whom is Baptism to be administered?

A. Baptism is to be administered to all those who actually profess repentance towards God (*Acts 2:38; Matt. 3:6; Mk. 16:16; Acts 8:12, 36-37; Acts 10:47-48*), and faith in our Lord Jesus Christ, and to none other.

77 Q. Are the infants of such as are professing to be baptized?

A. The infants of such as are professing believers are not to be baptized, because there is neither command nor example in the Holy Scriptures for their baptism (*Exod. 23:13; Prov. 30:6*).

78 Q. How is baptism rightly administered?

A. Baptism is rightly administered by immersion, or dipping the whole body of the person in water (*Matt. 3:16; Jn. 3:23*), in the name of the Father, and of the Son, and of the Holy Spirit, according to Christ's institution, and the practice of the apostles (*Matt. 28:19-20*), and not by sprinkling or pouring of water, or dipping some part of the body, after the tradition of men (*Jn. 4:1-2; Acts 8:38-39*).

79 Q. What is the duty of such as are rightly baptized?

A. It is the duty of such as are rightly baptized, to give up themselves to some particular and orderly Church of Jesus Christ (*Acts 2:47; 9:26; 1 Pet. 2:5*), that they may walk in all the commandments and ordinances of the Lord blameless (*Lk. 1:6*).

80 Q. What is the Lord's Supper?

A. The Lord's Supper is an ordinance of the New Testament, instituted by Jesus Christ; wherein, by giving and receiving bread and wine, according to his appointment, his death is shown forth (*1 Cor. 11:23-26*), and the worthy receivers are, not after a corporeal and carnal manner, but by faith, made partakers of his body and blood, with all his benefits, to their spiritual nourishment, and growth in grace (*1 Cor. 10:16*).

81 Q. What is required to the worthy receiving of the Lord's Supper?

A. It is required of them who would worthily partake of the Lord's Supper, that they examine themselves of their knowledge to discern the Lord's body (*1 Cor. 11:28-29*), of their faith to feed upon him (*2 Cor. 13:5*), of their repentance (*1 Cor. 11:31*), love (*1 Cor. 11:18-20*), and new obedience, (*1 Cor. 5:8*) lest coming unworthily, they eat and drink judgment to themselves (*1 Cor. 11:27-29*).

82 Q. What is meant by the words, "until he come," which are used by the apostle Paul in reference to the Lord's Supper?

A. They plainly teach us that our Lord Jesus Christ will come a second time; which is the joy and hope of all believers (*Acts 1:11 1 Thess. 4:16*).

Notes

CPSIA information can be obtained
at www.ICGtesting.com
Printed in the USA
LVHW111629180123
737311LV00005B/534